SCHOLASTIC

Geronimo Stilton ACADEMY

Comprehension Pawbook 2

Text by Geronimo Stilton
Based on the original idea by Elisabetta Dami
Illustrations by Piemme Archives

www.geronimostilton.com

© Atlantyca S.p.A. – via Leopardi 8, 20123 Milano, Italia – foreignrights@atlantyca.it

© 2015 for this Work in English language, Scholastic Education International (Singapore) Private Limited. A division of Scholastic Inc.
SCHOLASTIC and associated logos are trademarks and/or registered trademarks of Scholastic Inc.

Visit our website: www.scholastic.com.sg

First edition 2015

ISBN 978-981-4629-64-5

Stilton is the name of a famous English cheese. It is a registered trademark of the Stilton Cheese Makers' Association. For more information go to www.stiltoncheese.com

Welcome to the
Geronimo Stilton
ACADEMY

Well-loved for its humor, fascinating visuals and fun characters, the best-selling *Geronimo Stilton* series is enjoyed by children in many countries.

Research shows that learners learn better when they are engaged and motivated. The **Geronimo Stilton Academy: Comprehension Pawbook** series builds on children's interest in Geronimo Stilton. It makes learning more accessible, and increases learners' motivation to read and develop their reading comprehension skills.

The series comprises three levels:

Level 1	Level 2	Level 3
• predicting • inferring • sequencing • comparing and contrasting • recalling details and main ideas	All skills covered in Level 1 and • drawing conclusions • summarizing	All skills covered in Levels 1 and 2 and • giving reasons • stating opinions and point of view

Geronimo Stilton titles featured in this Pawbook:

© 2015 Scholastic Education International (S) Pte Ltd ISBN 978-981-4629-64-5

Motivating learners
Excerpts from *Geronimo Stilton* titles interest and encourage learners to read the rest of the story.

Developing comprehension skills
The 3-step format in each unit develops learners' comprehension skills and provides opportunities for independent learning.

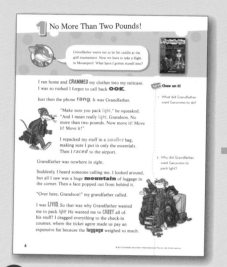
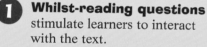

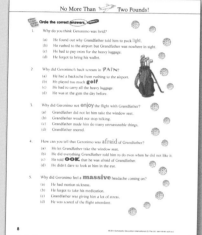

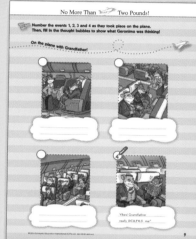

1 **Whilst-reading questions** stimulate learners to interact with the text.

2 **Comprehension questions** cover literal, inferential and higher-order reading skills for thorough understanding of the text.

3 **Graphic activities** develop learners' ability to translate what they have read and their visual text comprehension.

Extending vocabulary and understanding
Each double-page spread consists of a fun activity related to the preceding units to extend learning.

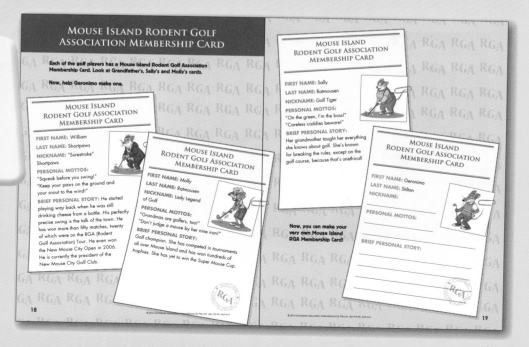

Contents

© 2015 Scholastic Education International (S) Pte Ltd ISBN 978-981-4629-64-5

1 No More Than Two Pounds!

Grandfather wants me to be his caddie at the golf tournament. Now we have to take a flight to Mouseport! What have I gotten myself into?

I ran home and **CRAMMED** my clothes into my suitcase. I was so rushed I forgot to call back **OOK**.

Just then the phone **rang**. It was Grandfather.

"Make sure you pack light," he squeaked. "And I mean really light, Grandson. No more than two pounds. Now move it! Move it! Move it!"

I repacked my stuff in a **smaller** bag, making sure I put in only the essentials. Then I **raced** to the airport.

Grandfather was nowhere in sight.

Suddenly, I heard someone calling me. I looked around, but all I saw was a huge **mountain** of luggage in the corner. Then a face popped out from behind it.

"Over here, Grandson!" my grandfather called.

I was **LIVID**. So that was why Grandfather wanted me to pack light! He wanted me to **CARRY** all of his stuff! I dragged everything to the check-in counter, where the ticket agent made us pay an expensive fee because the **luggage** weighed so much.

Chew on it!

1. What did Grandfather want Geronimo to do?

2. Why did Grandfather want Geronimo to pack light?

Excerpt from *The Giant Diamond Robbery*
(Originally published in Italy by Edizioni Piemme *Il Furto del Diamante Gigante*)

My back screamed in 𝐏𝐀𝐢𝐍. Just then we heard an **ANNOUNCEMENT** over the loudsqueaker:

"MR. VON KICKPAW IS WAITING FOR MR. STILTON AT BOARDING GATE C12!"

Cheese niblets! It was **OOK**! I rushed to the boarding gate. Kornelius was hiding behind a newspaper.

"I **need** to tell you something important...." he whispered.

But before he could continue, Grandfather dragged me away.

"No time for chitchatting, Grandson. My **FANS** are waiting. **WILLIAM SHORTPAWS, THE GOLF LEGEND**, cannot miss the plane!" he squeaked.

Grandfather pushed his way to the front of the boarding line. Two minutes later, we were in our seats. Grandfather took the window seat, which was fine with me. Did I mention I'm afraid of heights? After I checked my seat belt three times, we took off.

I should have known it wouldn't be an easy flight. Grandfather drove me 𝙲𝚁𝙰𝚉𝚈! ① First he insisted I ask the flight attendant for a glass of water with ice cubes shaped like **golf balls**. ② Then he wanted boiling **hot** coffee in his lucky mug. ③ And then he wanted the sports page of the newspaper! ④ Finally he ordered me to read a **book** called *The History of Golf for Dummies*. "I'll **QUIZ** you after the flight," he smirked.

I felt a **massive** headache coming on. What a trip!

No wonder the luggage weighed so much! Grandfather brought all his lucky charms along!

Wooden owl

Photo of Cheesita Lopez

A silver cup

Photo of Shortpaws's first golf instructor

Golf ball

Another silver cup

Key chain with number 18

3. Who is "The Golf Legend" Grandfather was talking about?

4. Why did Geronimo check his seat belt three times?

Excerpt from *The Giant Diamond Robbery*
(Originally published in Italy by Edizioni Piemme *Il Furto del Diamante Gigante*)

 Circle the correct answers.

1. Why do you think Geronimo was livid?

   (a) He found out why Grandfather told him to pack **light**.
   (b) He rushed to the airport but Grandfather was nowhere in sight.
   (c) He had to pay extra for the heavy luggage.
   (d) He forgot to bring his wallet.

2. Why did Geronimo's back scream in **PAiN**?

   (a) He had a backache from rushing to the airport.
   (b) He played too much **golf**.
   (c) He had to carry all the heavy luggage.
   (d) He was at the gym the day before.

3. Why did Geronimo not **enjoy** the flight with Grandfather?

   (a) Grandfather did not let him take the window seat.
   (b) Grandfather would not stop talking.
   (c) Grandfather made him do many unreasonable things.
   (d) Grandfather snored.

4. How can you tell that Geronimo was **afraid** of Grandfather?

   (a) He let Grandfather take the window seat.
   (b) He did everything Grandfather told him to do even when he did not like it.
   (c) He told **OOK** that he was afraid of Grandfather.
   (d) He didn't dare to look at him in the eye.

5. Why did Geronimo feel a **massive** headache coming on?

   (a) He had motion sickness.
   (b) He forgot to take his medication.
   (c) Grandfather was giving him a lot of stress.
   (d) He was scared of the flight attendant.

Excerpt from *The Giant Diamond Robbery*
(Originally published in Italy by Edizioni Piemme *Il Furto del Diamante Gigante*)

© 2015 Scholastic Education International (S) Pte Ltd ISBN 978-981-4629-64-5

Number the events 1, 2, 3 and 4 as they took place on the plane.
Then, fill in the thought bubbles to show what Geronimo was thinking!

On the plane with Grandfather!

_____

_____

_____

_____

_____

_____

4

Yikes! Grandfather _____

really **scares** me!"

Excerpt from *The Giant Diamond Robbery*
(Originally published in Italy by Edizioni Piemme *Il Furto del Diamante Gigante*)

The golf game has finally begun. Of all people, we are playing with Sally Ratmousen, my archenemy, and her grandmother, Molly Ratmousen.

Hole #1

Before I hit my ball, I held it up for everyone to see. This way, no one would **CONFUSE** my ball with the others.

Molly stomped up to me. She ripped the ball from my paws and examined it closely.

How **strange**!

Finally, I hit the ball. Then Grandfather hit his ball and Sally hit hers. When it was Molly's turn, she swung **HARD**. But instead of heading for the **GREEN**, the ball flew straight at me! It hit me in the head! **BONKKKKKKKKKK**!

I heard Sally's grandmother **SQUEAK**, "Geronimo Stilton can't continue the match! Team *Rodent's Gazette* must forfeit!"

Then I fainted. Grandfather sprang up. "We are **NOT** forfeiting!" he yelled. "Bring me some water!" A mouse from the clubhouse came **RUNNING**. Grandfather poured **freezing** water over me. I woke up in a flash. My fur was **SOAKED**. My head had a **lump**. And my knees felt **WEAK**.

"He's fine!" Grandfather insisted.

Molly giggled under her whiskers. How **strange**!

Chew on it!

1. Why would Molly examine the ball?

2. Why do you think Molly giggled?

10 Excerpt from *The Giant Diamond Robbery*
(Originally published in Italy by Edizioni Piemme *Il Furto del Diamante Gigante*)

Hole #2

At the second hole, my ball ended up in a **giant** tree. **Rats!**

Did I mention I'm **afraid** of heights?

MOLLY GIGGLED UNDER HER WHISKERS.
How strange!

Hole #3

At the third hole, my ball ended up in the middle of a cactus patch. I had to play with a million **THORNS** pricking me in the fur. I felt like a walking pincushion. **Youch!**

"Do it for The Rodent's Gazette!" Grandfather ordered.

I wondered why. Did she hate me that much? She sure was one very unusual mouse!

MOLLY GIGGLED UNDER HER WHISKERS.
How strange!

Hole #4

At the fourth hole, my ball ended up in a nest full of wasps. Wasps **BUZZED** all around me. When I hit the ball, they **ATTACKED**!

Oh, how had I gotten myself into such a **MESS**?

MOLLY GIGGLED UNDER HER WHISKERS.
How strange!

Hole #5

At the fifth hole, my ball ended up in something called a bunker. It's a ditch filled with sand. Every time I hit the ball, I dug a **deeper** hole.

Soon I was covered up to my neck!

MOLLY GIGGLED UNDER HER WHISKERS.
How strange!

3. Do you think Geronimo's golf game will improve?

4. Did Geronimo's golf game improve after the first hole? What do you think happens after Hole #5?

Excerpt from *The Giant Diamond Robbery*
(Originally published in Italy by Edizioni Piemme *Il Furto del Diamante Gigante*)

A. Circle the correct answers.

1. What happened to Geronimo at the first hole?

   (a) He hit his ball into the car park.

   (b) He fainted from the heat.

   (c) He was hit in the head by Molly's ball and fainted.

   (d) He was hit in the head by Molly's club and fainted.

2. Why did Grandfather throw **freezing** water on Geronimo?

   (a) To wake him up after he fainted

   (b) To cool him down

   (c) To make him wet

   (d) To help him feel better

3. Why did Geronimo think Molly hated him?

   (a) Every time he hit the ball, she would laugh at him.

   (b) Every time he talked to her, she would ignore him.

   (c) Every time he hit a bad shot, she would giggle.

   (d) Every time Grandfather scolded Geronimo, she would giggle.

4. Why do you think the writer repeats the line "Molly giggled under her whiskers. How **strange**!"?

   (a) To hint that she was up to something

   (b) To show that she was a mean mouse

   (c) To show that Geronimo was playing golf in a funny way

   (d) To hint that she had something in her whiskers

B. Geronimo thought that Molly behaved strangely. List what she did that was strange.

1. Before Geronimo hit his first shot, she _____.

2. When she hit her first shot, it _____.

3. Every time Geronimo hit a bad shot, she _____.

 Excerpt from *The Giant Diamond Robbery*
(Originally published in Italy by Edizioni Piemme *Il Furto del Diamante Gigante*)

© 2015 Scholastic Education International (S) Pte Ltd ISBN 978-981-4629-64-5

Imagine you're taking down notes to report on the golf game for the _Gazette_. Can you complete the notes below?

A terrible start to the day for Geronimo!

Hole #1:

- Geronimo gets hit _____

  _____

- He faints and it looked like his team would have to _____, but Grandfather _____

Hole #2:

- Geronimo hits his ball _____

- He has to climb up the tree to hit his next shot.

Hole #3:

- Geronimo's ball lands in _____

  _____

- As he hits the ball, the thorns _____

  _____

Hole #4:

- Geronimo hits his ball into _____

- The wasps _____

  _____

Hole #5:

- Geronimo's ball ends up _____

  _____

- He tries to hit the ball, but _____

  _____

© 2015 Scholastic Education International (S) Pte Ltd ISBN 978-981-4629-64-5

Excerpt from _The Giant Diamond Robbery_
(Originally published in Italy by Edizioni Piemme _Il Furto del Diamante Gigante_)

My golf game has been terrible since the first hole! Then, OOK told me something really strange.

Hole #14

At the fourteenth hole, I calculated our score. Despite everything, we were playing well. But when I told Grandfather, he slapped a paw over my mouth. "You'll JINX us!" he hissed.

I didn't want to do that, so I said, "Actually, we're playing TERRIBLY."

Grandfather looked ready to EXPLODE.

"Don't say that, either!" he shrieked.

I couldn't take it anymore. "So what CAN I say?" I asked.

"Nothing!" Grandfather thundered. "Be as quiet as a mouse!"

MOLLY GIGGLED UNDER HER WHISKERS. How strange!

Chew on it!

1. Why was Grandfather so angry with Geronimo?

Hole #15

At the fifteenth hole, when I stuck my paw in the hole to get my ball, a snake popped out. "Ahhhh!" I yelled.

 Excerpt from *The Giant Diamond Robbery*
(Originally published in Italy by Edizioni Piemme *Il Furto del Diamante Gigante*)

Luckily, the snake was rubber. I looked around to see who might be playing a prank.

MOLLY GIGGLED UNDER HER WHISKERS. How strange!

Hole #16

At the sixteenth hole, my ball was about to reach the hole, but then it made a TURN! It was as if my ball had a mind of its own!

MOLLY GIGGLED UNDER HER WHISKERS. How strange!

Hole #17

At the seventeenth hole, a bush started CALLING to me. I tried to ignore it, but it was very persistent. Then I saw OOK waving from behind the bush. Thank goodness I wasn't going CUCKOO!

OOK had some big news. "Molly Ratmousen is cheating! She's using a remote-control ball. Watch her carefully," he whispered.

When it was Molly's turn, her ball landed far away from the hole. *So much for the "Lady Legend of Golf," I thought.* Then I noticed her FUMBLING with something in her pocket. Was she about to pull out another poisoned cheese sandwich? I backed away. No way was I going to fall for that trick again! Then I heard a loud buzzing sound. BUZZ!

Slowly, the ball began rolling toward the hole. It turned right, then left, then ZIGZAGGED its way straight into the hole.

OOK was right. Molly Ratmousen was cheating!

2. Who do you think might have played the prank?

3. Geronimo's ball moved in a funny way. Do you think that there is something strange happening?

4. What do you think would happen next?

Excerpt from *The Giant Diamond Robbery*
(Originally published in Italy by Edizioni Piemme *Il Furto del Diamante Gigante*)

A. Circle the correct answers.

1. What do you think the word "jinx" means?

    (a) To bring bad luck to   (c) To make others angry

    (b) To help   (d) To make magic

2. What does the phrase "as quiet as a mouse" mean?

    (a) To be less quiet   (c) To talk normally

    (b) To be very quiet   (d) To talk loudly

3. Why did Geronimo think he was going CUCKOO?

    (a) He thought his ball was behaving weirdly.

    (b) He thought the bush was talking to him.

    (c) He could not believe that 00K was at the golf course.

    (d) He was unhappy that he was playing like a bird.

4. Why did Geronimo think "So much for the Lady Legend of Golf"?

    (a) Molly hit the ball badly and it ended up far away from the hole.

    (b) Molly played so well that she was legendary.

    (c) Molly hit the ball into the Lady Legend of Golf.

    (d) He was jealous of Molly's title as the Lady Legend of Golf.

B. The characters in the story are all quite different. Which of the following words best describes each of them, and why?

Observant	Superstitious	Cowardly	Sneaky

Character	Description	Reason
Grandfather		
Geronimo		
Molly		
00K		

 Excerpt from *The Giant Diamond Robbery*
(Originally published in Italy by Edizioni Piemme *Il Furto del Diamante Gigante*)

It was clear that Molly Ratmousen was cheating! Can you figure out her secret? Look at the way Geronimo's ball moves and how Molly's ball moves. How did she do it?

Now, look at the pictures below. Did you manage to guess Molly's secret?

HAVE YOU FIGURED OUT MOLLY RATMOUSEN'S SECRET?

MOLLY WAS USING A

This was my original ball. . . . Notice the number and the brand!

ULTRATOP BRAND

SERIES NO. 131313

This ball does not make buzzing sounds and does not vibrate!

This was the ball that had replaced mine. . . .

ULTRATRIK BRAND

SERIES NO. 83795648

This ball emits a buzzing sound!

Excerpt from *The Giant Diamond Robbery*
(Originally published in Italy by Edizioni Piemme *Il Furto del Diamante Gigante*)

MOUSE ISLAND RODENT GOLF ASSOCIATION MEMBERSHIP CARD

Each of the golf players has a Mouse Island Rodent Golf Association Membership Card. Look at Grandfather's, Sally's and Molly's cards.

Now, help Geronimo make one.

MOUSE ISLAND RODENT GOLF ASSOCIATION MEMBERSHIP CARD

FIRST NAME: William

LAST NAME: Shortpaws

NICKNAME: "Surestroke" Shortpaws

PERSONAL MOTTOS:

"Squeak before you swing!"
"Keep your paws on the ground and your snout to the wind!"

BRIEF PERSONAL STORY: He started playing way back when he was still drinking cheese from a bottle. His perfectly precise swing is the talk of the town. He has won more than fifty matches, twenty of which were on the RGA (Rodent Golf Association) Tour. He even won the New Mouse City Open in 2006. He is currently the president of the New Mouse City Golf Club.

MOUSE ISLAND RODENT GOLF ASSOCIATION MEMBERSHIP CARD

FIRST NAME: Molly

LAST NAME: Ratmousen

NICKNAME: Lady Legend of Golf

PERSONAL MOTTOS:

"Grandmas are golfers, too!"
"Don't judge a mouse by her nine iron!"

BRIEF PERSONAL STORY:
Golf champion. She has competed in tournaments all over Mouse Island and has won hundreds of trophies. She has yet to win the Super Mouse Cup.

Excerpt from *The Giant Diamond Robbery*
(Originally published in Italy by Edizioni Piemme *Il Furto del Diamante Gigante*)

© 2015 Scholastic Education International (S) Pte Ltd ISBN 978-981-4629-64-5

MOUSE ISLAND RODENT GOLF ASSOCIATION MEMBERSHIP CARD

FIRST NAME: Sally

LAST NAME: Ratmousen

NICKNAME: Golf Tiger

PERSONAL MOTTOS:

"On the green, I'm the boss!"
"Careless caddies beware!"

BRIEF PERSONAL STORY:
Her grandmother taught her everything she knows about golf. She's known for breaking the rules, except on the golf course, because that's unethical!

Now, you can make your very own Mouse Island RGA Membership Card!

MOUSE ISLAND RODENT GOLF ASSOCIATION MEMBERSHIP CARD

FIRST NAME: Geronimo

LAST NAME: Stilton

NICKNAME:

_____

PERSONAL MOTTOS:

_____

_____

BRIEF PERSONAL STORY:

_____

_____

_____

_____

_____

© 2015 Scholastic Education International (S) Pte Ltd ISBN 978-981-4629-64-5

Excerpt from *The Giant Diamond Robbery*
(Originally published in Italy by Edizioni Piemme *Il Furto del Diamante Gigante*)

4 I'm Dragging From Jet Lag

Finally back from a trip and all I wanted to do was to rest. What could possibly happen?

It was a *hot* summer day and I was exhausted. I had just returned from a trip to the Restful Tails Resort in the Swiss Alps and I was dragging from jet lag.

So much for feeling restful! I could barely keep my eyes **open**!

Don't get me wrong — I love visiting Switzerland. I mean, who wouldn't love the place where they invented Swiss cheese? But flying back and forth between time zones had left me with a terrible case of jet lag.

Do you know what **JET LAG** is?

It's something that happens to rodents when they travel by plane and cross from one time zone into another. Your body clock feels like it's one time, but the local clock says it's another. It makes your insides feel like curdled cheese!

First your head gets **heavy**, then your eyes begin to **close**, then your stomach gets upset, and then your tail droops. Plus, the worst part is that at night, your body thinks it's still morning, so you can't fall asleep!

 **Chew on it!**

1. Why didn't Geronimo feel rested?

2. Do you think jet lag happens to humans too?

TIME ZONES

The Earth is divided into twenty-four sections called time zones. Every section corresponds to an hour. When you travel across continents, your watch must be adjusted an hour for every section you cross. If you go east, the hour is added, and if you go west, the hour is subtracted. So if it is eight p.m. in London, it is three p.m. in New York.

Excerpt from *The Mystery in Venice*
(Originally published in Italy by Edizioni Piemme *Il mistero della gondola di cristallo*)

© 2015 Scholastic Education International (S) Pte Ltd ISBN 978-981-4629-64-5

Cheese niblets! I hate jet lag!

This is one of the many reasons that I have never loved to travel. In fact, I guess you could say my two most favorite places in the world are my cozy **mouse hole** and my office at *The Rodent's Gazette.*

Oh, how rude. I haven't even introduced myself. My name is Stilton, *Geronimo Stilton*, and I am the publisher of *The Rodent's Gazette*, the most famouse newspaper on Mouse Island.

Anyway, what was I saying?

Ah, yes, I was telling you how much **I WAS DRAGGING FROM JET LAG**!

But luckily I had a plan.

I was going to put my anti–jet lag remedy into action: a warm bath, pajamas, slippers, a cup of tea, and right to bed!

But as soon as I started to relax, the telephone rang.

I got out of the tub grumbling. **❶** First, I couldn't find my bath towel, so I grabbed one that was way too small. **❷** Next, I headed toward the living room dripping soapy water everywhere. Meanwhile, the telephone kept ringing and ringing. Rats! It was giving me a **mouse-sized headache!** **❸** As I raced for the phone, I slipped on a puddle and fell on my tail. **Ouch!** **❹** I tried to get up but lost my balance and fell forward right on my snout. **THUMP!** **❺** Finally, I reached the phone and stammered, **"H-h-hello?"**

3. Do you think Geronimo likes to travel?

4. What do you think happened to Geronimo when the phone rang?

Excerpt from *The Mystery in Venice*
(Originally published in Italy by Edizioni Piemme *Il mistero della gondola di cristallo*)

A. Circle the correct answers.

1. Why did Geronimo expect to be well-rested after his trip?

    (a)   He visited the Restful Tails Resort which was supposed to be restful.

    (b)   He had lots of Swiss cheese.

    (c)   He would have slept a lot on the plane.

    (d)   He had stayed in an expensive hotel in Switzerland.

2. Why was Geronimo suffering from **JET LAG**?

    (a)   His travels took him to different time zones.

    (b)   He had to travel in a jet plane.

    (c)   He experienced time travel.

    (d)   His travels made him sick.

3. Why would someone suffering from jet lag not be able to sleep at night?

    (a)   They would get a stomach upset and be too uncomfortable.

    (b)   They would suffer from headaches and not be able to sleep.

    (c)   They would feel like they are still traveling.

    (d)   Their body would think that it is morning and time to be awake.

B.   What was Geronimo going to do to get rid of his jet lag? List the steps that he hints at. Use your own words.

1. _____

    _____

2. _____

    _____

3. _____

    _____

4. _____

    _____

 Excerpt from *The Mystery in Venice*
(Originally published in Italy by Edizioni Piemme *Il mistero della gondola di cristallo*)   ISBN 978-981-4629-64-5

Geronimo's plans were rudely interrupted. When he tried to get to the phone, lots of things happened. Explain why the series of events happened?

1

Geronimo got out of the tub grumbling because _____

_____

The towel he took was too small because _____

_____

2

He dripped water everywhere when he _____

_____

3

There were puddles of water everywhere so he _____

_____

4

He fell on his snout as _____

_____

before he finally reached the phone!

5

Excerpt from *The Mystery in Venice*
(Originally published in Italy by Edizioni Piemme *Il mistero della gondola di cristallo*)

I couldn't believe who it was that called me on the phone. It must be my lucky day!

From the other end of the line, a **sweet** voice responded, "Hi, G, you sound funny. Am I bothering you?"

It was Petunia Pretty Paws, *the rodent of my dreams*!

Chew on it!

I should have said something clever, charming, and unforgettable.

Instead, I turned purple with embarrassment (good thing I don't have a videophone), my tongue felt like a stale **BRICK** of cheddar, and I spit out **silly sentences**.

"Yes—I mean no. That is, what I mean is . . . I am Geronimo and you no **disturb** me. I mean, you're not . . . You would never, that is—"

She interrupted me, sounding worried. "Are you sure you're feeling **all right**?"

I touched the bump on my head. Then I rubbed the bruise on my tail and felt my whiskers droop. "I have **JET LAG**, a **bruised tail**, and a terrible **headache**!" I wailed.

She was silent for a minute. "Oh, too bad," she said kindly. "I wanted to invite you—"

At that moment my spirits **soared**. "Okay, I'll come! I'm feeling better already!" I squeaked. There was no way

1. How do you think Geronimo answered Petunia's question?

2. Why would having a videophone be embarrassing?

3. Why do you think the conversation breaks off here?

 Excerpt from *The Mystery in Venice*
(Originally published in Italy by Edizioni Piemme *Il mistero della gondola di cristallo*)

 ISBN 978-981-4629-64-5

I was going to miss spending time with Petunia.

"Great! I'll be by to get you in ten minutes," she replied.

I hung up the phone and smiled. Yes, I still felt AWFUL from the jet lag. My head was **pounding**. My stomach hurt. But I didn't care. I was too HAPPY! Petunia had invited me to go out with her! My heart was **BEATING** a mile a minute and I began to skip around the room, shouting **HOORAY!**

Then, **SUDDENLY**, I realized that I hadn't asked her where she wanted to invite me. . . .

Did she want to invite me to take a romantic stroll at sunset?

Or did she want me to see a documentary about nature with her?

Or maybe she wanted to have a candlelit dinner?

I chewed my whiskers. How was I supposed to dress?

With my mind racing, I began to try on all different combinations of clothes at **warp speed**. Soon shirts and pants and ties and socks littered the room . . . but nothing looked good!

Right at that moment, the doorbell rang: Ding-dong!

I was so excited I ran to open the door without thinking about how I was dressed.

4. How do you think Geronimo dressed in the end?

Excerpt from *The Mystery in Venice*
(Originally published in Italy by Edizioni Piemme *Il mistero della gondola di cristallo*)

The Rodent of 🌹 My Dreams!

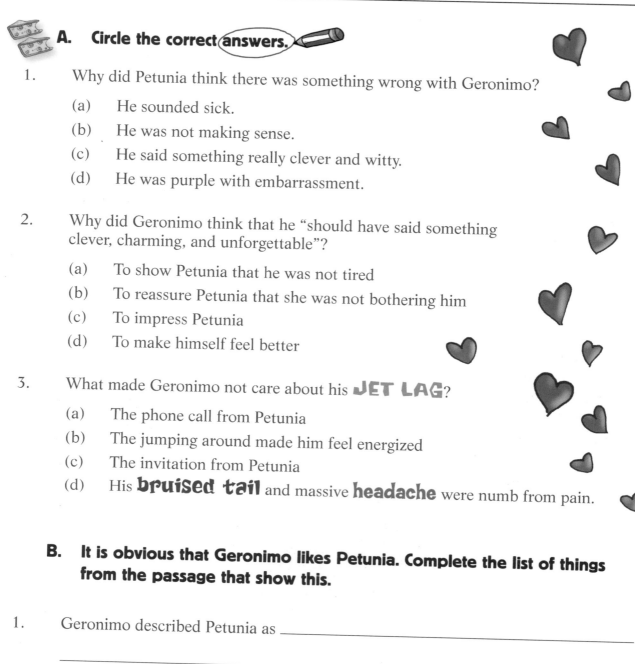

A.   Circle the correct answers.

1.   Why did Petunia think there was something wrong with Geronimo?

   (a)   He sounded sick.

   (b)   He was not making sense.

   (c)   He said something really clever and witty.

   (d)   He was purple with embarrassment.

2.   Why did Geronimo think that he "should have said something clever, charming, and unforgettable"?

   (a)   To show Petunia that he was not tired

   (b)   To reassure Petunia that she was not bothering him

   (c)   To impress Petunia

   (d)   To make himself feel better

3.   What made Geronimo not care about his **JET LAG**?

   (a)   The phone call from Petunia

   (b)   The jumping around made him feel energized

   (c)   The invitation from Petunia

   (d)   His **bruised tail** and massive **headache** were numb from pain.

B.   It is obvious that Geronimo likes Petunia. Complete the list of things from the passage that show this.

1.   Geronimo described Petunia as _____

   _____

2.   When talking to Petunia, he _____

3.   He was so happy that she invited him out, he _____

   _____

4.   He tried on different _____ for the date.

Excerpt from *The Mystery in Venice*
(Originally published in Italy by Edizioni Piemme *Il mistero della gondola di cristallo*)

The Rodent of 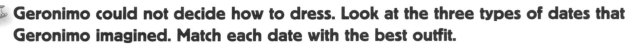 My Dreams!

Geronimo could not decide how to dress. Look at the three types of dates that Geronimo imagined. Match each date with the best outfit.

 romantic stroll   candlelit dinner    watching a documentary

A Elegant and sophisticated?   **B** Sporty and casual?   **C** Normal, like every day?

Now, look at what Geronimo wore in the end. What do you think happened?

_____
_____
_____
_____
_____
_____
_____
_____
_____
_____
_____

Do you think Geronimo would get his wish and go on a romantic date with Petunia? Why or why not?

© 2015 Scholastic Education International (S) Pte Ltd ISBN 978-981-4629-64-5 (Originally published in Italy by Edizioni Piemme Il mistero della gondola di cristallo)

Excerpt from The Mystery in Venice

After our visit to the flea market, Petunia gave me a glittering gondola as a present. What mystery would it contain?

We climbed back into Thea's sports car and headed for home. As we drove, the crystal gondola kept **lighting up** and playing its annoying song. The music was so **LOUD**, mice on the streets shot me disgusted looks as we passed by.

How **humiliating**!

When we arrived at my mouse hole, I said good-bye and ran inside. I couldn't wait to get out of my *ridiculous* outfit and put on my regular clothes.

After I got changed, I looked around for somewhere to put the gondola. Since it was a **gift** from Petunia, I couldn't hide it in the back of a drawer somewhere, or under the bed, or in a closet. I needed to leave it in plain sight. I started wandering around the house, looking for the perfect spot.

Umm . . . on the mantel?
No, it wouldn't fit.
On the COFFEE TABLE?
No, it clashed with the carpet.
On the nightstand?
No, if that annoying song went off, I'd never get to sleep.

Right at that moment the doorbell rang. I ran to open it, but the door burst open and I was **KNOCKED** over by my cousin Trap. The crystal gondola fell to the floor, breaking into a thousand pieces.

Chew on it!

1. What did Geronimo think of the gondola?

2. What do you think happened next?

Excerpt from *The Mystery in Venice*
(Originally published in Italy by Edizioni Piemme *Il mistero della gondola di cristallo*)

CRASHHH!!!

I tried to put the pieces back together as tears fell from my eyes. Even though the gondola was hideous, it was a **gift** from Petunia! I was devastated!

"Trap, how could you!" I wailed. "That was a present from **Petunia**!"

"What's the big deal?" Trap chuckled. "It's not like she's your girlfriend or anything."

3. What do you think of Trap's reaction to Geronimo?

I **GLARED** at him. My cousin knows that I have a crush on **Petunia** and I am too shy to tell her. Of course, that doesn't stop him from teasing me about it.

"She bought me that **CRYSTAL GONDOLA** at the flea market today," I squeaked. "Now that you broke it, she'll think I didn't like it. I'll never be able to tell her I like her, and it's all your fault!"

He giggled. "You should thank me, Cousin!" he replied. "From the little that is left, I can really tell that thing was **hideous**!"

I ignored him and started picking up *TINY* pieces of crystal in hopes of fixing the gondola.

It was then that I realized that a piece of *rolled-up* paper had been stuck inside the gondola. I unrolled it and read these words:

I gulped. It was a dramatic call for help. I had to do something **immediately**!

4. What might Geronimo's next step be?

"Look at this!" I squeaked, shoving the paper under my cousin's nose. "Someone is in **DANGER** and needs help! Maybe it's a damsel in distress!"

A. Circle the correct answers.

1. Why did Geronimo want to put the gondola "in plain sight"?

    (a) It was a beautiful piece of art.

    (b) It was an expensive item he bought for himself.

    (c) It was a priceless antique he found in the flea market.

    (d) It was a **gift** from Petunia and he wanted to show her that he treasured it.

2. Did the gondola really break into "a thousand pieces"? What do you think the phrase means?

    (a) It means that the gondola did not break.

    (b) It means that the gondola broke into many tiny pieces.

    (c) It means that Geronimo's heart broke into many pieces.

    (d) It means that the gondola was made up of a thousand pieces.

3. Why was Geronimo devastated when the gondola broke?

    (a) He really liked the gondola.

    (b) He was upset that he had to piece it back again.

    (c) He was upset that it was broken and he had to clean up.

    (d) It was precious to him because it was a gift from **Petunia**.

4. What did Trap think Geronimo should thank him for?

    (a) Teasing him

    (b) Fixing the ugly gondola

    (c) Breaking the ugly gondola

    (d) Telling Petunia that Geronimo likes her

B. Complete the following sentence.

1. From the picture below and the phrase, "damsel in distress", we can tell that Geronimo imagines himself as

    _____

Excerpt from *The Mystery in Venice*
(Originally published in Italy by Edizioni Piemme *Il mistero della gondola di cristallo*)

© 2015 Scholastic Education International (S) Pte Ltd ISBN 978-981-4629-64-5

Trap is Geronimo's cousin and is very different from him. He can be described as sarcastic, annoying and careless. Give evidence from the passage to support this description.

Sarcastic

Evidence from passage

_____

_____

_____

_____

_____

Annoying

Evidence from passage

_____

_____

_____

_____

_____

Careless

Evidence from passage

_____

_____

_____

_____

Excerpt from *The Mystery in Venice*
(Originally published in Italy by Edizioni Piemme *Il mistero della gondola di cristallo*)

Geronimo's adventure to find the person in need of help led him to the shop in Venice that made the glass gondolas. He was hired as an apprentice but he was not very good at it!

Working with Glass

Glassblowing is a method that is used by artisans to shape glass. You place the end of a metal pole in melted glass and then you blow into the other end of the pole. The glass inflates and is shaped while it is still soft. Another method makes use of pliers to shape the melted glass.

Based on the text above, write a set of instructions for Geronimo to follow.

Working With Glass

1. First, _____

   _____

2. Then, blow _____

   _____

3. The glass will _____

   _____

4. Shape _____ while _____

   or use _____ to shape the melted glass.

Excerpt from *The Mystery in Venice*
(Originally published in Italy by Edizioni Piemme *Il mistero della gondola di cristallo*)

© 2015 Scholastic Education International (S) Pte Ltd   ISBN 978-981-4629-64-5

Unfortunately, Geronimo was not very good at following the instructions. Match the descriptions of what happened to him with the correct pictures.

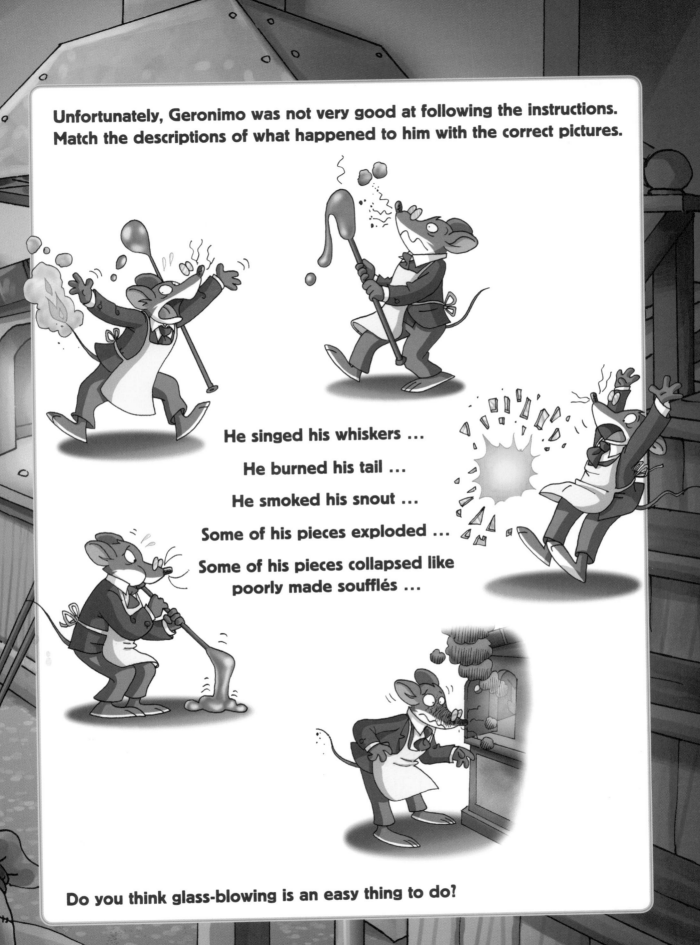

He singed his whiskers …

He burned his tail …

He smoked his snout …

Some of his pieces exploded …

Some of his pieces collapsed like poorly made soufflés …

Do you think glass-blowing is an easy thing to do?

Excerpt from *The Mystery in Venice*
(Originally published in Italy by Edizioni Piemme *Il mistero della gondola di cristallo*)

7 An Alarming Pilot

I was on my way to Shell Island to learn scuba diving but I brought the wrong suitcase! Instead of my hot weather stuff, I brought my cold weather stuff! What was I going to do?

"Don't worry, G!" Petunia consoled me. "It was a simple mix-up. And this means that when we get to the island, we're going **shopping**!"

I sighed. Oh, how I hate **shopping**!

"Come on, *let's move it* — our plane's about to leave!" Petunia said.

If I knew what was waiting for me on the plane, I would have turned around and gone to the mountains! There were no regular flights to Shell Island, so the TV station Petunia was working for had organized a private flight.

The problem, however, was not the plane, but the pilot! He looked like an aviator from the last century with his leather helmet and pair of goggles covered with dust. He also had a very loud voice.

"WELCOME ABOARD!" he shouted as soon as we boarded. "MY NAME IS FLASH PIROUETTE, AND I AM CAPTAIN OF THIS AIRCRAFT. BUCKLE YOUR SEAT BELTS AND BRING YOUR SEAT TO AN UPRIGHT POSITION! WE ARE ABOUT TO TAKE OFF!"

"He knows what he's doing, right?" I asked Petunia.

"He sure does!" she answered with a *smile*. She continued excitedly, "He's so good, he's won the **MOUSE ISLAND STUNT FLYING CHAMPIONSHIP** twice!"

 Chew on it!

1. Do you think Petunia likes shopping?

2. How do you think the plane ride went?

3. Would you trust a pilot who looked like that?

34

Excerpt from *The Enormouse Pearl Heist*
(Originally published in Italy by Edizioni Piemme *Il mistero della perla gigante*)

As if he had heard her, Flash began **ZIGZAGGING** between the clouds,

up and down and up and down.

YIKES! Even if I wasn't such a scaredy-mouse, I think that might have been too much for me!

Finally, we cleared the clouds and the airplane settled into a normal flight path. After an hour, we came in sight of Shell Island.

"There it is!" exclaimed Petunia, pointing to a tiny **emerald-green** spot shining in the middle of the **dark-blue** South Mousific Ocean. It didn't look inhabited other than one small settlement.

"I can't see the **RUNWAY** for the plane," I said worriedly.

"Of course you can't! There isn't any!"

"Wh-what do you mean there's no runway? How are we going to **land**?"

"We'll land in the **WATER** and we'll get to shore with the airplane's life raft!" Petunia explained.

"**WHAAAAAAAAAAAT? HEEEEEEEELP!**" I yelled, terrified.

Suddenly, the plane veered to the side and headed straight toward the ocean at full speed.

YIKES! I wanted to live!

Luckily, despite what I predicted, Flash landed the plane *gently* and smoothly. We got to shore in no time at all.

4. How do you think they would land the plane?

5. Was the plane ride as you expected?

Excerpt from *The Enormouse Pearl Heist*
(Originally published in Italy by Edizioni Piemme *Il mistero della perla gigante*)

Circle the correct answers.

1. What was Petunia's solution to Geronimo's problem?

    (a) To lend him her clothes
    (b) To go back and bring the correct suitcase
    (c) To buy new clothes when they get to Shell Island
    (d) To borrow clothes from the people at Shell Island

2. Do you think a lot of people go to Shell Island? Why or why not?

    (a) Yes, because it is a popular place for scuba diving.
    (b) No, because there are no regular flights that go there.
    (c) Yes, because private planes go to Shell Island.
    (d) No, because the TV station where Petunia worked did not want to go there to film.

3. Why do you think Geronimo asked if the pilot knew what he was doing?

    (a) He did not trust the pilot.
    (b) He thought the plane was too old.
    (c) He was worried that the pilot was deaf.
    (d) He was afraid of flying.

4. What do you think Geronimo predicted?

    (a) He predicted that they would crash into the ocean.
    (b) He predicted that they would crash into Shell Island.
    (c) He predicted that they would have to make an emergency landing on the RUNWAY.
    (d) He predicted that they would land safely on the water.

 Excerpt from *The Enormouse Pearl Heist*
(Originally published in Italy by Edizioni Piemme *Il mistero della perla gigante*)

© 2015 Scholastic Education International (S) Pte Ltd ISBN 978-981-4629-64-5

Flash Pirouette is definitely not your typical pilot. In the Venn Diagram below, compare and contrast Flash with a typical commercial pilot. Use the helping words and phrases in the box.

Wears a leather helmet
Does not wear goggles
Wears dust-covered goggles
Shouts to be heard in the plane
Flies the plane in a zigzag way
Wears a pilot's uniform

Flies commercial flights
Flies a plane
Takes part in stunt competitions
Flies a normal flight path
Uses a speaker to be heard

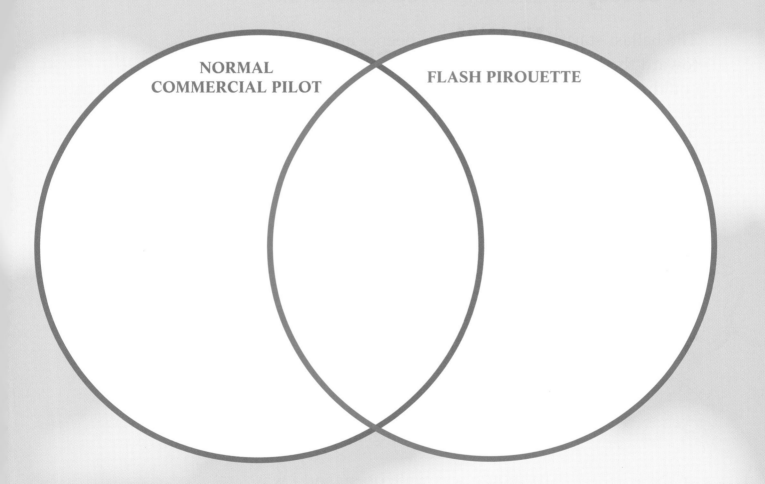

NORMAL COMMERCIAL PILOT

FLASH PIROUETTE

Excerpt from *The Enormouse Pearl Heist*
(Originally published in Italy by Edizioni Piemme *Il mistero della perla gigante*)

On my scuba diving trip with Simon and Petunia, just when I thought I could finally learn to enjoy myself, things started to go wrong!

A second later, one of the flippers *slipped* from my paw and I was left **kicking** sideways like a fish with one fin. Oh, **why** did these things always happen to me?

The ballast started **DRAGGING** me deeper and deeper toward the bottom. I wanted to **SCREAM** but I couldn't, and no one noticed me.

Simon was leading the way. And Petunia was so intent on **FILMING** that nothing would have distracted her.

 **Chew on it!**

Headlines flashed before my eyes: *Publisher's Deadly Dive! Geronimo Stilton: The Story of a Drowned Rat!*

The water was becoming **dark** and murky. It was so **spooky**. Could things get any worse?

Then they did. Suddenly, I noticed a sparkling light below me. I looked down and saw the gigantic **blue** fish!

Its mouth was wide open, and I was **TUMBLING** right into it!

AAAAAAAAAAAAAAAAAAAAAAAAAAAAAAAHHHH!

1. What do you think was going through Geronimo's mind?

2. What do you think happened next?

Excerpt from *The Enormouse Pearl Heist*
(Originally published in Italy by Edizioni Piemme *Il mistero della perla gigante*)

© 2015 Scholastic Education International (S) Pte Ltd ISBN 978-981-4629-64-5

Desperately, I began fumbling with the weight belt, trying to unbuckle it, but my paws were trembling so much I was getting nowhere. I sank DEEPER and DEEPER.

Thundering cattails! The enormouse jaws of the blue fish were closing in on me! I was about to become a mouthful of furry fish food!

I looked up for the last time and I thought I could see the light from Petunia's camera coming toward me. *Good-bye, sweet Petunia! I* sobbed *to myself. Good-bye, family! Good-bye, world!*

But when I looked down again, I saw the most amazing sight. It was an enormouse blue oyster, and its shell was completely open. In its center sat a huge, glowing pearl.

I couldn't believe my eyes! Uncle Grayfur was right! I hadn't seen a gigantic blue fish — I had discovered the famouse giant oyster, also known as **The Eye of the Ocean**!

Unfortunately, as soon as I hit bottom, I kicked up a CLOUD of sand, and the shell snapped itself shut as if it wanted to protect its treasure.

A minute later, Simon also arrived. Simon tried to open the blue pod with his bare paws, but the oyster's shell was completely sealed.

He tried to force it with a rock, but still it wouldn't open.

I was glad Petunia *motioned* for him to stop. The oyster was so *beautiful*. It would be awful if he ruined it.

3. How do you think Geronimo was feeling?

Excerpt from *The Enormouse Pearl Heist*
(Originally published in Italy by Edizioni Piemme *Il mistero della perla gigante*)

 **Circle the correct answers.**

1. Why would no one notice Geronimo was sinking to the bottom?

    (a)   He was behind them and they could not see him.

    (b)   He did not want to look stupid and **SCREAM** for help.

    (c)   They were too preoccupied with the blue oyster.

    (d)   They thought that he could scuba-dive so they left him on his own.

2. Which two items were causing Geronimo to sink?

    (a)    (b)

    (c)    (d)

3. How can we tell that Geronimo was sinking further down to the bottom?

    (a)   He started to see bright lights.

    (b)   They had to dive down after him.

    (c)   The water was starting to get **dark** and murky.

    (d)   There were ghosts in the water and it was getting **spooky**.

4. Why did Geronimo start saying goodbye to Petunia and to the world?

    (a)   He thought he was going to drown.

    (b)   He thought he was going to get sucked into the oyster.

    (c)   He was trying to catch Petunia's attention.

    (d)   He was afraid she would go up to the boat first.

5. Why do you think the **shell** snapped shut?

    (a)   It was trying to protect itself.

    (b)   It was trying to eat Geronimo but it missed.

    (c)   It was playing with Geronimo.

    (d)   It was trying to prevent Simon from taking the pearl.

 Excerpt from *The Enormouse Pearl Heist*
(Originally published in Italy by Edizioni Piemme *Il mistero della perla gigante*)

© 2015 Scholastic Education International (S) Pte Ltd   ISBN 978-981-4629-64-5

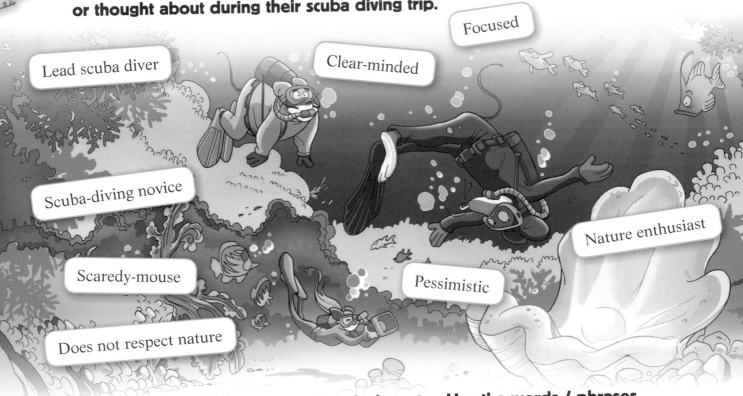
A. Match the descriptions to the characters. Think about what each of them did or thought about during their scuba diving trip.

Focused

Lead scuba diver

Clear-minded

Scuba-diving novice

Nature enthusiast

Scaredy-mouse

Pessimistic

Does not respect nature

B. Complete a short description of each character. Use the words / phrases above to help you.

Simon Provolone	During the dive, Simon was the _____. He _____ and tried to force the oyster open. If Petunia had not stopped him, he would have _____.
Petunia Pretty Paws	This pretty mouse is so _____ on her filming that she _____. She is also _____ and decisive. She knew that she had to stop Simon from destroying the oyster.
Geronimo Stilton	Geronimo is a _____ and he gets frightened by everything. He is _____ and imagines the worst! He is clearly a _____ and does not know much about scuba-diving.

Excerpt from *The Enormouse Pearl Heist*
(Originally published in Italy by Edizioni Piemme *Il mistero della perla gigante*)

41

Finally the oyster was retrieved and packed safe and sound. Professor Fishywhiskers from the New Mouse City Aquarium was going to transport it there and exhibit the rare find!

By the time the oyster was packed up safe and sound, it was *dusk*. The professor wanted to leave immediately, but Captain Crooked Paw refused to sail.

"We'll spend the **NIGHT** at the dock, then leave first thing in the morning," he insisted.

Later at dinner, Professor Fishywhiskers stroked his beard **nervously**. "I'm not sure why, but I have a **bad** feeling," he confessed. "I think it would be a good idea if we all keep an **eye** on the oyster tonight."

Petunia and I volunteered to stay on the boat and guard the **oyster** while Aunt Sweetfur stayed with Benjamin and Bugsy Wugsy in the hotel.

After dinner, we went back to the laboratory ship to spend the night. I have to admit, I wasn't crazy about the idea of **SLEEPING** on a boat. Did I mention that I get **seasick**?

Oh, well. At least the boat was staying at the dock. I was just thinking that maybe I shouldn't have eaten that second **loaded** cheddarburger, when the professor waved us into his cabin.

"I'm worried!" he whispered. "The oyster is in **DANGER**,

Chew on it!

1. What do you think the Professor was worried about?

2. Why did Geronimo wish he had not eaten that second burger?

Excerpt from *The Enormouse Pearl Heist*
(Originally published in Italy by Edizioni Piemme *Il mistero della perla gigante*)

and I may be as well. If something happens to me, I want you to know how to open **The Eye of the Ocean** without harming it."

"Don't be silly, Professor," Petunia reassured him.

But the professor insisted. He whispered the **SECRET** in our ears. Petunia and I looked at each other, surprised.

"Now that I told you, I feel better," said the professor. "Go and take your watch **GUARDING** the oyster. We'll say good-bye tomorrow morning."

Petunia and I settled ourselves on the ship's deck wrapped in **WOOLEN** blankets. Above us, the sky was filled with stars.

For a while, I forgot about the oyster. It was a beautiful night, and I was with the mouse of my **DREAMS**! Too bad I was tired. Before long, I was snoring away. When I woke up at dawn, I was drooling. How embarrassing!

Even worse — when I went to check on the oyster, I discovered the professor had **disappeared**!

3. What do you think happened to the professor?

Excerpt from *The Enormouse Pearl Heist* (Originally published in Italy by Edizioni Piemme *Il mistero della perla gigante*)

Circle the correct answers.

1. What did Professor Fishywhiskers want to do straight after the **oyster** was packed?

    (a) He wanted to have dinner.
    (b) He wanted to go to sleep.
    (c) He wanted to set off immediately.
    (d) He wanted to spend the night at the docks.

2. What did Professor Fishywhiskers suggest they do during the night?

    (a) Spend the night stargazing
    (b) Keep watch over the oyster
    (c) Guard him when he went to sleep
    (d) Set sail so that they can reach the aquarium in the morning

3. Why did the professor think that he might be in **DANGER** as well?

    (a) Only he had the pearl
    (b) Only he knew where the oyster was kept
    (c) Only he could communicate with the oyster
    (d) He knew the secret of opening the oyster without hurting it.

4. Why did Geronimo temporarily forget about the oyster?

    (a) He was too seasick to think about it.
    (b) He was too worried about the professor.
    (c) He was enjoying his night with Petunia.
    (d) He was thinking of what the professor had told them.

5. What evidence tells us that the professor is a smart and cautious mouse? Tick all the relevant answers.

    ☐ He suspected that someone would try to steal the oyster and told them to watch over it.
    ☐ He would stroke his beard nervously.
    ☐ He told Petunia and Geronimo the secret to opening the oyster.
    ☐ He wanted to leave immediately.
    ☐ He wanted to say good-bye to them the next morning.
    ☐ He disappeared without a trace.

Excerpt from *The Enormouse Pearl Heist*
(Originally published in Italy by Edizioni Piemme *Il mistero della perla gigante*)

© 2015 Scholastic Education International (S) Pte Ltd ISBN 978-981-4629-64-5

A. What do you think happened? Number the events 1, 2, 3 and 4 as they are likely to have taken place.

GETTING THE OYSTER

WORRIED PROFESSOR SHARES SECRET TO OPENING OYSTER

IMMERSE OYSTER IN TANK PACK IN WOODEN CRATE CUSHION WITH PACKING MATERIALS

SLEEPING ON THE SHIP WATCHING OVER OYSTER

B. Now, use the pictures and helping words to write a short summary of the events. End your summary with the disappearance of the Professor.

_____

_____

_____

_____

_____

_____

© 2015 Scholastic Education International (S) Pte Ltd ISBN 978-981-4629-64-5

Excerpt from *The Enormouse Pearl Heist*
(Originally published in Italy by Edizioni Piemme *Il mistero della perla gigante*)

Detective Work

Play detective! After Geronimo found The Eye of the Ocean, many things happened. Look at some of the clues on these two pages. Can you answer the questions to figure out what happened?

CLUE 1

AFTER GERONIMO DISCOVERED THE PEARL, HE TOLD THE OTHERS ABOUT IT. GERONIMO WANTED TO WRITE ABOUT IT AND PETUNIA AIR WHAT SHE HAD FILMED. THEN GERONIMO'S LAPTOP AND PETUNIA'S CAMERA WERE STOLEN. WHY WOULD THEIR BELONGINGS GET STOLEN?

CLUE 2

GERONIMO DISCOVERS A GOLD EARRING ON HIS BED. WHO WEARS GOLD EARRINGS? (HINT: LOOK AT THE PICTURES BELOW.)

CLUE 3

THE SHIP FROM THE AQUARIUM ARRIVES, GERONIMO SEES THE CAPTAIN AND SIMON PROVOLONE WHISPERING TO EACH OTHER. WHAT COULD THEY BE WHISPERING ABOUT?

Who did it? Tick the boxes of those you suspect to be involved. Why do you suspect them?

Excerpt from *The Enormouse Pearl Heist*
(Originally published in Italy by Edizioni Piemme *Il mistero della perla gigante*)

© 2015 Scholastic Education International (S) Pte Ltd ISBN 978-981-4629-64-5

CLUE 4

THE OYSTER WAS READY TO BE TRANSPORTED TO THE AQUARIUM BUT THE PROFESSOR GOT KIDNAPPED. WHO WOULD KNOW THAT ONLY THE PROFESSOR KNEW THE SECRET TO OPENING THE OYSTER?

CLUE 5

SOMETHING STRANGE WAS HAPPENING. COMPARE THE PICTURES OF THE OYSTER AND PACKING CRATES IN THE PICTURES. DO YOU NOTICE THE DIFFERENCES? HOW DID THEY TRY TO STEAL THE OYSTER?

The cats on Cat Island were wasting electricity and going broke paying their bills. One day, the power supply gets cut off. What will Catardone, the king of Cat Island do?

"I'll tell you what's going on!" Catardone **hissed**. "Everyone has been wasting so much electricity and fuel around here that we have run out of **MONEY** to pay our bills! So until one of you figures out a way to get us some **GOLD**, I've taken matters into my own paws and turned off the power!"

Gasps and sad meowing rose from the crowd.

"Oh, don't be such a bunch of kittens!" Catardone scolded. "We can use *candles* instead of lightbulbs, and instead of driving everywhere, we can walk. It's great exercise." Then the king added under his breath, "Though, of course, I will be pushed in the **ROYAL CARRIAGE**, because I'm already in great shape."

Then he stood up, tripped over his own tail, and **TUMBLED** down the stairs. **BONZO FeLiX** and **Boots**, his trusty assistants, rushed to help him.

Chew on it!

1. How do you think the other cats would react to the news?

2. Why does Catardone excuse himself from walking? Do you believe him?

Excerpt from *The Golden Statue Plot*
(Originally published in Italy by Edizioni Piemme *Attacco alla statua d'oro!*)

3. Do you think Regina Redfur's name suits her? Why?

At that moment, one of the scientists from the Catlab stood up. It was Dr. Regina Redfur.

"Your Excellency, I hate to complain, but you turned off the **electricity** just as we were purrfecting a new **anti-flea portable shower system.** . . ." she began.

"Oh yeah? Well, try getting **stuck** in an elevator for an hour!" interrupted Simon Scarsnout.

"At least your **FAVORITE** scallop-flavored ice cream didn't **melt** in your freezer!" Tomcat Pat whined.

"Who cares about ice cream?" Hillary Hotpaws snorted. "I was in the middle of baking a gourmet **CATNIP** casserole!"

"Enough!" Catardone shrieked. "I can't take any more of this whining! I don't care about your **shower** system, your elevator, or your **melted** ice cream! I just told you, we've got to figure out a way to pay our energy bills, or invent some other way to make electricity. Until then, I'm keeping you in the **D A R K**!"

"There goes movie night," Tomcat Pat sniffled.

But Catardone wasn't listening. He had sidled up to Hillary Hotpaws. "Maybe you could make that catnip casserole over an open **FIRE**," he suggested. Just the thought of some tasty catnip had the king **drooling** like a rabid stray cat.

Excerpt from *The Golden Statue Plot*
(Originally published in Italy by Edizioni Piemme *Attacco alla statua d'oro!*)

A. Circle the correct answers.

1. What was the reason Catardone gave for turning off the power?

    (a) He wanted to see what it was like to be powerless.

    (b) He wanted to play hide and seek with the other cats.

    (c) He wanted to use up the electricity and fuel on Cat Island.

    (d) He wanted his advisors to figure out a way to get GOLD to pay for the electricity bills.

2. What were the scientists at Catlab trying to do?

    (a) They were researching an anti-flea portable shower system.

    (b) They were trying to find ways to make gold.

    (c) They were stuck in the elevator for an hour.

    (d) They were finding new ways to save electricity.

3. From the reactions of the cats, which of the following sentences is true?

    (a) They were used to the lack of electricity.

    (b) They were used to being in good shape.

    (c) They did not know what to do about Catardone.

    (d) They were used to wasting electricity and did not know what to do without it.

B. What were some of the solutions that Catardone gave to overcome the lack of power? Complete the table below.

Problem	Solution
Lightbulbs cannot be used.	
They cannot drive around.	
Baking cannot be done.	

Excerpt from *The Golden Statue Plot*
(Originally published in Italy by Edizioni Piemme *Attacco alla statua d'oro*)

© 2015 Scholastic Education International (S) Pte Ltd ISBN 978-981-4629-64-5

Look at the pictures below. What problems would the cats face with the power and fuel taken from them? Write them next to the pictures.

Excerpt from *The Golden Statue Plot*
(Originally published in Italy by Edizioni Piemme *Attacco alla statua d'oro!*)

Catardone brought his advisors together to try to find a solution to their electricity problems. What would these sneaky cats come up with?

Catardone **clapped** his paws for attention.

"Silence!" he ordered. Then he looked around the room.

"I didn't bring all you scientists here just to gripe. I brought you all here so you'd get your **TAILS** in gear and find a solution to our problem. So stop *meowing* and start moving!"

The scientists looked at one another blankly. No one had any brilliant ideas.

But just then, Dr. Redfur **MEOWED** excitedly. She turned to Catardone.

"**I've got it**, Your Excellency, Your Furryness, Your Hefty Highness — I mean, Catardone," she announced.

The king narrowed his eyes as the cat began digging through her bag.

First, she pulled out a pair of **PAJAMAS**, then a bathrobe, a toothbrush, some **toothpaste**, a brush, fluffy socks, and a bar of soap from her bag.

"I never know how long these **URGENT** meetings are going to last," she explained matter-of-factly.

Finally, she found what she was looking for. It was a map of **MOUSE ISLAND**!

"Here is the **solution!**" Dr. Redfur exclaimed.

The rest of the cats stared at the map, confused.

 **Chew on it!**

1. What were the scientists doing?

2. What kind of impression does this give you of Dr. Redfur?

Excerpt from *The Golden Statue Plot*
(Originally published in Italy by Edizioni Piemme *Attacco alla statua d'oro!*)

© 2015 Scholastic Education International (S) Pte Ltd ISBN 978-981-4629-64-5

"Uh, what are we going to do with a map, Dr. Redfur?" asked Bonzo.

"Are we going to BURN it and use it as fuel?" asked Boots, scratching his head.

Dr. Redfur laughed. "Don't be an alley cat," she chided. She pointed a claw at the port of NEW MOUSE CITY.

"You see this?" she asked.

"Yes, it's Mousey Liberty," responded Kitty.

"Exactly!" said Dr. Redfur. "According to my scientific calculations, it is the only treasure that we should be able to reach without the use of a high-powered boat. We can take *The Black Hurricane*. All we have to do is get to the island and STEAL the statue."

"And we'd want to STEAL an old statue because . . ." Bonzo murmured, bewildered.

"Because . . . that old statue is made of GOLD!" Dr. Redfur finished, smiling proudly.

3. Why couldn't they have used a high-powered boat?

At the mention of gold, Tersilla's ears perked up. She loved gold almost as much as she loved **tuna fish**!

Then Oscar asked, "But are you sure the statue is made of gold?"

Dr. Redfur's fur ruffled. "What kind of question is that? Of course I am sure the statue is made of gold! We are scientists and, therefore, we have scientific proof. The statue is YELLOW, right? And gold is YELLOW, isn't it? So the statue is made of gold!" she insisted.

Oscar and the twins stared at Dr. Redfur skeptically. What kind of scientific proof was that? What happened to research? What happened to evidence?

4. Do you think Oscar believes her? Why?

© 2015 Scholastic Education International (S) Pte Ltd ISBN 978-981-4629-64-5   Excerpt from *The Golden Statue Plot*
(Originally published in Italy by Edizioni Piemme *Attacco alla statua d'oro!*) **53**

A Golden  Statue

Circle the correct answers.

1. Why does the writer use words like "**TAILS**" and "meowing"?

    (a) The characters are cats which have tails and meow.

    (b) To make the characters funnier

    (c) Because the writer likes cats

    (d) To show how irritating the characters are

2. What reason did Dr. Redfur give for having so many things in her bag?

    (a) She was being hygienic.

    (b) She was being prepared for long meetings.

    (c) She was being funny and trying to show off a new magic trick.

    (d) She was going to stay over at her friend's house.

3. What do you think Dr. Redfur meant by the phrase "Don't be an alley cat"?

    (a) She was trying to tell Boots not to be so silly.

    (b) She was trying to tell Boots not to stay in alleys.

    (c) She was trying to tell Boots that he was an alley cat.

    (d) She was trying to show off.

4. What **scientific proof** did Dr. Redfur give to prove the statue was made of **GOLD**?

    (a) She showed them her scientific research.

    (b) She showed them secret letters from Mouse City.

    (c) She compared the color of gold to the color of the statue.

    (d) She heard it from someone at Mouse City.

5. Is Dr. Redfur's proof good? Why or why not?

    (a) Yes, because the color of gold and the statue are the same.

    (b) No, because she did not conduct research or have evidence to show the statue was made of gold.

    (c) Yes, because Dr. Redfur is a famous scientist.

    (d) No, because Oscar and the twins did not believe her.

 Excerpt from *The Golden Statue Plot*
(Originally published in Italy by Edizioni Piemme *Attacco alla statua d'oro!*)

© 2015 Scholastic Education International (S) Pte Ltd ISBN 978-981-4629-64-5

A Golden Statue

Look at the pictures and descriptions of the different Statues of Liberty below. What are some of the similarities and differences?

STATUES OF LIBERTY

IN NEW YORK . . .

The Statue of Liberty is located in the United States of America, in New York, very close to the island of Manhattan. It is a gift that the French gave to the United States in 1886, to celebrate the hundredth anniversary of American independence (in 1876).

. . . IN PARIS . . .

To celebrate the hundredth anniversary of the French Revolution in 1889, the United States gave a gift to France: a bronze copy of the original statue. This statue is in Paris. It is only 37 feet tall, while the original is 151 feet tall.

. . . AND IN NEW MOUSE CITY!

The New Mouse City Statue of Liberty (also known as Mousey Liberty) was constructed after the Great War of Rats and Cats. The statue holds a piece of cheese in one paw, and, in the other, a book with the words of the New Mouse City anthem written on it. The seven points on its crown symbolize freedom.

Similarities	Differences

© 2015 Scholastic Education International (S) Pte Ltd   ISBN 978-981-4629-64-5

Excerpt from *The Golden Statue Plot*
(Originally published in Italy by Edizioni Piemme *Attacco alla statua d'oro!*)

Catardone and his advisors had to devise a plan to steal Mousey Liberty from the New Mouse City. What plan would they come up with?

The next day, Catardone, Bonzo, Boots, Tersilla, and the rest of the king's advisors headed to the secret meeting place in the underground offices of **The Cat Island Most Wanted Headquarters**. It's a place where they study all the ways to catch mice like (gulp!) me, *Geronimo Stilton*!

"Remember, this mission needs to be top secret," Catardone reminded everyone as they reached the soundproof office door.

But before they could put in the password, a cat in slippers and a robe came **shuffling** out, complaining, "This place stinks! The water in the shower is **ice-cold**!"

The king **arched** his back. "What is the meaning of this?! What is this stray doing in our secret headquarters?!" he shrieked.

Boots **CHEWED** his pawnail. "Um, it's nothing to worry about, Your Felineness," he soothed. "I thought it would be a good idea to rent out the space. You said we are **LOW** on cash."

"You mean **anyone** can come stay here?" Catardone demanded.

"No, of course not, not anyone," Boots explained. "I mean, they need to pay up first. And then I give them the **PASSWORD**."

 **Chew on it!**

1. Why do you think the place is soundproof?

2. What do you think that cat was doing there?

 Excerpt from *The Golden Statue Plot*
(Originally published in Italy by Edizioni Piemme *Attacco alla statua d'oro!*)

The king gasped. "The p-p-password?" he mumbled. Then he **fainted**.

Two hours later, the king woke up. By then his advisors had already organized the plan to sail to New Mouse City and steal the GOLDEN statue.

Later that day, Catardone laid out the plan to his crew. First they would prepare the king's ship, *The Black Hurricane*, for the voyage. Then, once they arrived at the port of New Mouse City, they would **knock** the statue down with cannonballs. Then they would tie it to the ship and **DRAG** it back to Fort Feline.

"It's a purrfect plan! We sail at dawn!" the king announced.

Meanwhile, **scout**, *Kitty*, and **OSCAR** had listened to Catardone's plan also, thanks to a two-way radio *hidden* in the Most Wanted Headquarters.

3. What does this tell you about the secret headquarters?

"What a strange plan," remarked Oscar.

"It's not just **strange**, Uncle, it's fur-raising. Dragging the statue through the **SEA** will damage the ocean floor and hurt a lot of animals!" Kitty wailed.

"We've got to tell *Geronimo Stilton*," Scout said. "But how do we reach him?"

…Just then, Oscar had an idea. You see, Oscar's eldest daughter, Samantha, loved reading my books. In fact, she even traveled to **Niagara Falls**, a place I described in one of my bestsellers.

"I know Sammy communicates with that literary rat all the time," Oscar explained. "She sends **messages** to him using a carrier pigeon. And I know just where to find the old bird."

4. What do you think the cats would do?

"Great idea, Uncle!" the kittens **Meowed** happily.

Excerpt from *The Golden Statue Plot*
(Originally published in Italy by Edizioni Piemme *Attacco alla statua d'oro!*)
57

Circle the correct answers.

1.   Why did Catardone want to go to the secret headquarters to discuss the plan?

    (a)   The plan was supposed to be top secret.

    (b)   There was no other place with electricity.

    (c)   He liked the secret headquarters.

    (d)   He wanted to research how to catch mice at the same time.

2.   What was Boots' solution to the lack of money?

    (a)   To steal Mousey Liberty

    (b)   To rent out the secret headquarters

    (c)   To reduce the amount of electricity used

    (d)   To raise money by selling the PASSWORD to the secret headquarters

3.   Why did Catardone faint?

    (a)   He was shocked that Boots had given out the password to the secret headquarters.

    (b)   He was angry with Boots for not selling the password.

    (c)   He was shocked that there was a password.

    (d)   He was angry that he forgot the password.

4.   Why was Kitty upset about the plan to steal Mousey Liberty?

    (a)   The plan would cause damage to the ocean floor and hurt a lot of animals.

    (b)   The plan would use too much electricity.

    (c)   The plan would cause the cats' fur to rise.

    (d)   She was upset that she was not involved in the plan.

5.   What did the kittens think was a great idea?

    (a)   To stop the other cats from stealing Mousey Liberty

    (b)   To send a warning message to Geronimo using a carrier pigeon

    (c)   To take *The Black Hurricane* to New Mouse City

    (d)   To steal Mousey Liberty

Excerpt from *The Golden Statue Plot*
(Originally published in Italy by Edizioni Piemme *Attacco alla statua d'oro!*)

© 2015 Scholastic Education International (S) Pte Ltd ISBN 978-981-4629-64-5

The P-P-  Password?

Look at the pictures below. Use the pictures and the text to complete the list of instructions that Catardone gives to his crew.

1 WE LEAVE!

We must _____
_____
_____.

Then, we will sail to the port of New Mouse City.

2 WE FIRE!

When we reach _____
_____
_____.

Make sure we bring enough cannonballs.

3 WE STEAL!

Finally, we will _____
_____
_____
_____
_____
_____
_____.

Do you think this is a good plan? What could go wrong?

Excerpt from *The Golden Statue Plot*
(Originally published in Italy by Edizioni Piemme *Attacco alla statua d'oro*)

Saving Energy

Read some of Geronimo's practical advice to save energy. Can you think of other ways? Add on your ideas on the next page.

Practical Advice to Save ENERGY

Sometimes, saving energy is just a matter of a few small tricks. Here's some advice!

→ Take advantage of daylight as best you can.

→ Always turn off lights you aren't using.

→ Use energy-efficient lightbulbs.

→ Dust your lamps periodically; a clean lamp gives off more light.

→ Rediscover activities that don't use electricity, such as board games and outdoor games.

→ Don't leave electronic devices (computers, televisions, DVD players, speakers, etc.) in standby mode. Turn them off.

→ Keep doors and windows closed when heat or air-conditioning is on in your house.

→ If it's cold outside, wear a sweatshirt or sweater indoors so you don't have to turn up the heat.

→ If it's hot out, instead of turning on the air conditioner, draw the shades or close the blinds to help keep your house cooler.

HELP SAVE ENERGY!

Excerpt from *The Golden Statue Plot* (Originally published in Italy by Edizioni Piemme Attacco alla statua d'oro)

© 2015 Scholastic Education International (S) Pte Ltd ISBN 978-981-4629-64-5

More Ways to Save Energy

Excerpt from *The Golden Statue Plot*
(Originally published in Italy by Edizioni Piemme *Attacco alla statua d'oro*)

Answers

Section 1
Unit 1
Pages 6–7
Whilst-reading questions:
1. Grandfather wanted Geronimo to pack light.
2. Grandfather wanted Gernomino to carry all his stuff.
3. Himself
4. He was afraid of flying and wanted to ensure he was safe.

Page 8
1. a   2. c   3. c   4. b   5. c

Page 9

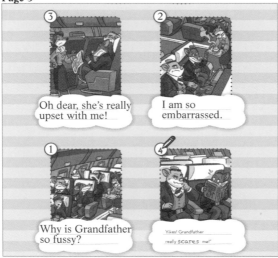

Unit 2
Pages 10–11
Whilst-reading questions:
1. Suggested answers: She was trying to make sure that Geronimo was using a normal ball. OR She was trying to do something to Geronimo's ball.
2. Molly giggled because she found it funny that Geronimo got hit in the head.
3. No, because his game started badly. OR Yes, because it was only the first hole and things can get better.
4. No, it did not. His game is likely to get worse after Hole #5.

Page 12
A 1. c   2. a   3. c   4. a
B 1. examined his ball.
    2. hit Geronimo in the head.
    3. would giggle.

Page 13
Hole #1 • in the head.
            • forfeit; threw freezing water on him.
Hole #2 • into a giant tree.
Hole #3 • the middle of a cactus patch.
            • prick him in the fur.
Hole #4 • a nest full of wasps.
            • buzzed around him and then attacked when he hit the ball.
Hole #5 • in a bunker.
            • only ends up digging a deeper hole.

Unit 3
Pages 14–15
Whilst-reading questions:
1. He felt that Geronimo's comments on how well they were playing would bring them bad luck.
2. It might have been Molly.
3. Yes, because it acted like it had a mind of its own.
4. Accept all reasonable answers.

Page 16
A 1. a   2. b   3. b   4. a
B

Character	Description	Reason
Grandfather	Superstitious	He was angry with Geronimo for saying things that would bring them bad luck.
Geronimo	Cowardly	When he thought he had found a snake in Hole #15, he yelled in fright.
Molly	Sneaky	She fumbled with something in her pocket and suddenly her ball started rolling toward the hole.
OOK	Observant	He was able to tell that Molly was cheating by watching her.

Page 17
Molly was using a remote-controlled ball.

Activity 1
Pages 18–19
Accept all reasonable answers.

Section 2
Unit 4
Pages 20–21
Whilst-reading questions:
1. He had jet lag.
2. Suggested answer: Yes, we too would feel the effects of traveling across different time zones.
3. No, because he hates jet lag.
4. Accept all reasonable answers.

Page 22
A 1. a   2. a   3. d
B 1. He would take a warm bath.
    2. He would then put on his pajamas and wear his slippers.
    3. He would have a cup of tea.
    4. He would go to bed.

Page 23
1. • the phone rang just as he was starting to relax.
    • he couldn't find his bath towel.
2. ran into the living room.
3. slipped and fell on his tail.
4. he lost his balance while trying to get up

Unit 5
Pages 24–25
Whilst-reading questions:
1. He probably said something very silly.
2. A videophone would show Geronimo as he really was, wet and wearing a small towel. He would not have wanted Petunia to see him that way.

3. It shows Geronimo interrupting Petunia and how eager he is to go to wherever she is inviting him to.
4. He probably dressed in a very strange way.

Page 26
A 1. b   2. c   3. c
B 1. "the rodent of my dreams".
     2. wanted to say something clever, charming, and unforgettable.
     3. didn't care about his jet lag, his pounding head, or his stomachache.
     4. combinations of clothes

Page 27
1. [romantic stroll]   C
2. [candlelit dinner]   A
3. [documentary]   B
• Geronimo probably could not decide what to wear and ended up combining different types of clothes.
• Accept all reasonable answers.

Unit 6
Pages 28–29
Whilst-reading questions:
1. He did not like the gondola.
2. Accept all reasonable answers.
3. Trap was teasing Geronimo.
4. He might look for the writer of the note.

Page 30
A 1. d   2. b   3. d   4. c
B 1. a knight in shining armor

Page 31
Suggested answers.
Sarcastic: He tells Geronimo that he should thank him for destroying the ugly gondola.
Annoying: He purposely teases Geronimo about his crush.
Careless: He barges into Geronimo's house and knocks him over.

Activity 2
Pages 32–33
1. First, place the end of a metal pole in melted glass.
2. Then, blow into the other end of the pole.
3. The glass will inflate.
4. Shape the glass while it is still soft or use pliers to shape the melted glass.

Section 3
Unit 7
Pages 34–35
Whilst-reading questions:
1. Yes, because she told Geronimo that they could go shopping to solve the problem of the mixed up suitcases.
2. It probably went horribly.
3. Accept all reasonable answers.
4. Suggested answer: They would land the plane on water.
5. Accept all reasonable answers.

Page 36
1. c   2. b   3. a   4. a

Page 37

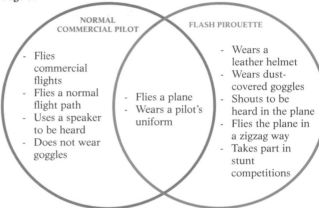

NORMAL COMMERCIAL PILOT
- Flies commercial flights
- Flies a normal flight path
- Uses a speaker to be heard
- Does not wear goggles

- Flies a plane
- Wears a pilot's uniform

FLASH PIROUETTE
- Wears a leather helmet
- Wears dust-covered goggles
- Shouts to be heard in the plane
- Flies the plane in a zigzag way
- Takes part in stunt competitions

Unit 8
Pages 38–39
Whilst-reading questions:
1. He thought he was going to drown.
2. Accept all reasonable answers.
3. He was feeling desperate.

Page 40
1. d   2. a   3. a   4. a   5. a

Page 41
A Simon: lead scuba diver; does not respect nature
    Petunia: focused; clear-minded; nature enthusiast
    Geronimo: scuba-diving novice; scaredy-mouse; pessimistic
B Simon Provolone: lead diver; does not respect nature; ruined the oyster
    Petunia Pretty Paws: focused; would not be distracted by anything; clear-minded
    Geronimo Stilton: scaredy-mouse; pessimistic; novice scuba-diver

Unit 9
Pages 42–43
Whilst-reading questions:
1. The Professor was worried about the oyster being stolen.
2. He gets seasick and would have to spend the night on the boat so having the second burger might make him feel worse.
3. Suggested answer: He got kidnapped.

Page 44
1. c   2. b   3. d   4. c
5. Relevant answers are the first, third and fourth sentences.

© 2015 Scholastic Education International (S) Pte Ltd   ISBN 978-981-4629-64-5

Page 45

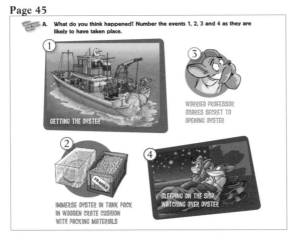

A. What do you think happened! Number the events 1, 2, 3 and 4 as they are likely to have taken place.

1. GETTING THE OYSTER
2. IMMERSE OYSTER IN TANK PACK IN WOODEN CRATE CUSHION WITH PACKING MATERIALS
3. WORRIED PROFESSOR SHARES SECRET TO OPENING OYSTER
4. SLEEPING ON THE SHIP WATCHING OVER OYSTER

They retrieved and packed the oyster safely. The Professor wanted to leave immediately but the Captain refused. Petunia and Geronimo volunteered to spend the night on the boat to guard the oyster. Afraid that he was in danger, the Professor told Petunia and Geronimo how to open the oyster without harming it. The next day, the Professor disappeared.

Activity 3
Pages 46–47
Clue 1: Someone was trying to prevent news of the oyster from getting out.
Clue 2: The Provolones
Clue 3: They were probably planning something bad.
Clue 4: Those involved in transporting the oyster.
Clue 5: One of the oysters has 4 sections instead of 5. The crate the oyster was packed in has changed. The word "FRAGILE" is spelled differently. They probably exchanged the crates and tried to steal the real oyster.

The Provolones and the Captain were probably the ones who tried to steal the oyster.

Section 4
Unit 10
Pages 48–49
Whilst-reading questions:
1. Suggested answer: They would probably be shocked and upset.
2. He says that he's already in great shape and doesn't need the exercise. No, because he then tripped over his own tail and tumbled down the stairs.
3. Suggested answer: Yes, because she has bright red fur.

Page 50
A   1. d   2. a   3. d
B

Problem	Solution
Lightbulbs cannot be used.	Use candles instead.
They cannot drive around.	They can walk.
Baking cannot be done.	Cook over an open fire.

Page 51

	They were not able to continue their research.
	Their ice-cream would melt.
	They would not be able to use power speedboats.
	They would not be able to fly planes.
	They would not be able to use their computers and laptops.

Unit 11
Pages 52–53
Whilst-reading questions:
1. They were complaining and whining.
2. Accept all reasonable answers.
3. The electricity had been switched off and they had no fuel to power the boat.
4. No, because she did not give them any scientific proof or evidence.

Page 54
1. a   2. b   3. a   4. c   5. b

Page 55
Similarities:
- All three statues symbolize independence and freedom.
- All three statues are called Statues of Liberty.
- The statues look similar with one hand outstretched and the other holding a book.

Differences:
- The statues in New York and Paris were gifts but Mousey Liberty was constructed after the Great War.
- The statues in New York and Paris feature a woman but Mousey Liberty shows a mouse.

Unit 12
Pages 56–57
Whilst-reading questions:
1. So that secrets cannot be heard from outside the room
2. He was staying there.
3. It is not very secret or secure.
4. They will send a message to Geronimo Stilton by carrier pigeon.

Page 58
1. a   2. b   3. a   4. a   5. b

Page 59
1. prepare the king's ship, *the Black Hurricane*, for the journey.
2. the port of New Mouse City, we will knock the statue down with cannonballs.
3. tie the statue to the ship and drag it back to Fort Feline.

Accept all reasonable answers.

Activity 4
Pages 60–61
Accept all reasonable answers.

© 2015 Scholastic Education International (S) Pte Ltd   ISBN 978-981-4629-64-5